WHAT WIVES & GIRLFRIENDS REALLY WANT

JACK CARPENTER
WITH DENNIS LOWERY

WISHBOOK | What Wives and Girlfriends Really Want

JACK CARPENTER
WITH DENNIS LOWERY

Copyright © 2017. All rights reserved. No part of this book may be reproduced or transmitted in any form or by any means, electronic or mechanical, including photocopying, recording or by any information storage and retrieval system, without written permission from the author, except for brief quotations as would be used in a review.

ISBN 9781937592738

All statements of fact, opinion, or analysis expressed are those of the author and do not reflect the official positions or views of the publisher. Nothing in the contents should be construed as asserting or implying authentication of information or endorsement of the author's views. This book and subjects discussed herein are designed to provide the author's opinion about the subject matter covered and is for informational purposes only.

DEDICATION

This book was inspired by and is dedicated to my lovely bride of 21 years, the accomplished Ms. Ariane Whittemore.

Acknowledgments

I want to acknowledge the good men from all walks of life who have been the inspiration for this book. These men are earth's salt and do their best to support families, careers, friends, faith, and country.

On occasion, a little extra effort and encouragement are appropriate to make life with our wife or girlfriend more fulfilling, exciting and enjoyable. This book attempts to be an instrument of that extra effort and encouragement.

TABLE OF CONTENTS

ABOUT THE TITLE	I
FOREWORD	1
INTRODUCTION	2
SUGGESTION ONE — It's Supposed to Be Fun, Make It So	8
SUGGESTION TWO—Listen	16
SUGGESTION THREE — Don't Interrupt	27
SUGGESTION FOUR — Respect and Lots of It	38
SUGGESTION FIVE — Compliment Every Day	45
SUGGESTION SIX — Don't Be a Jerk	55
SUGGESTION SEVEN — How to Fight Fair	65
SUGGESTION EIGHT — Get Off the Couch	75
SUGGESTION NINE — SPACE (The Final Frontier)	85
SUGGESTION TEN — Live Like You Are Courting	91
CLOSING	99
A CALL TO ACTION	103
AFTERWORD	106
ABOUT THE AUTHOR	111

"As You Wish..."
—Westley, in *The Princess Bride* by William Goldman

ABOUT THE TITLE

Once his book's content (the narrative) was about 95% where Jack wanted it, he and I talked about moving beyond the working title. We knew—and had received independent feedback (from our wives and their friends)—that the original working title wasn't appealing. So, I gave Jack my Naval Gunfire Support mission analogy. [NGFS deals with a ship's shore bombardment to support amphibious landing operations, counter-battery fire, etc.] It's one that proves true with each and every book or story I've worked on. I told him:

"Jack, with working titles and cover designs, it's like gunfire support where it's not unusual to fire long... shoot short... then adjust to get on target and fire for effect." He and I are surface warfare Navy veterans, so he got what I meant. And so, it was. We knew we needed to get on target with the right title. We continued talking about the book, and that led to a stream of conscious bit from me on how I perceived the book's content and scope. That line of discussion became a train of thought—for me—that triggered a memory. It went like this:

"When I was a young boy, I would occasionally spend a weekend with my great-grandmother. Now, I grew up relatively poor, and my great-grandmother had lived a hard-scrabble life. She had raised her kids and helped raise her grandchildren through the breadth and depth of the Depression era and still to that day (this was in 1971) had little in the way of luxuries or even comforts that we today take for granted. She had never—to my knowledge—owned a TV but did have an old radio. In the evenings she would sit, chew tobacco, rock in her chair with the radio dialed in on a country and western station at low volume, and read. Two things only (every night): The Old Testament and the Montgomery Ward catalog.

"The Bible was big and heavy, black leather scuffed and scarred... it looked as old as she was (about 80 at that time). I'd watch her from the old couch that smelled of dog—even though she didn't own one—as I read my own book. After about an hour, she'd glance at the side table at the catalog. After the third or so glance, she'd shut the Bible, setting it on her lap (it would go with her when she grew too tired to read; the Bible was always kept on the small table next to her bed). And she'd pick up the catalog.

"Now, my Big Granny (we called her that though she was a tiny lady, just barely 5 feet tall and maybe 110 pounds at the most) never—ever—smiled. It's not that she was mean; it was just that she had lived a harsh life that had rubbed away any softness. She might not have laughed or smiled around me (or anyone that I ever saw), but I could always count on her cooking my favorite foods (skillet-fried chicken and fresh biscuits with gravy, peach cobbler, and other good stuff). She had a cast-iron skillet as big as a 1950s Cadillac hubcap that felt like it weighed 30 pounds; she'd handle it like it was nothing and could cook a complete meal in just it. That's how she showed love.

"Anyway, the first few times seeing her with the catalog, I noticed that after turning—slowly—several of the pages, that her face had lost its tension and the edges of her lips curved slightly up. The barest hint of a smile was on her face. Sometimes she'd stop rocking and lean forward to hold an open page under the table light. She'd squint at it, and sometimes the smile would grow, then with the briefest of a head shake she'd lean back and turn the page.

"I finally asked her, 'Big Granny, what are you reading?'

"'Not reading... just looking,' her lips had straightened out. Big Granny wasn't much of a talker, you had to go after—chase down—any conversation you hoped to have with her.

"'Looking at what?'" I wanted to know what it could be that would make her face soften.

"She stopped rocking, 'Come here, boy.'

"'Yes'm,' I hopped off the couch and in three steps stood beside her.

"'This,' she pointed to the catalog that now rested open on her lap, 'is my wish book.'

"I thought of the story of Aladdin and the lamp (I'd read *One Thousand and One Nights* earlier that summer). 'What's a wish book?'

"She looked up at me, and for a moment I thought she might give me that little bit of a smile. 'It's got all the things I wish I could have, but never did... likely never will.'"

Now, that's a memory I had all but forgotten. As Jack and I talked about his book—its theme and what he wanted to convey in it—I thought about Big Granny and her wish book. As my stream about it ran out and tapered off, Jack stopped me. "Back up. What did you call it? Wish book?"

"Yeah," I replied. "It was her wish book."

"That's it!" Jack said. "That could be a great title for the book!"

I mulled that over for a moment and agreed with him. As Jack and I chatted, a wish of my own had come to me: She's long ago passed on, but I wished that back then I'd been able to give my Big Granny some of the things she wanted. I also realized that she'd lived alone for a very long time. That made me think about how blessed I am to not want for things and how important it is to have someone by your side in life. Someone to share the ups and downs, the good and the bad. Someone to hold that wants you to, and that embraces you in return. Someone to have fun with. Someone to grow old with.

I came back to real-time in our conversation and to what Jack and I were still talking about and had another realization. He has created the perfect wish book for women (and frankly, I think for men too). In an entertaining—and often quirky, humorous way—it shows men how to get things right with the women in their lives; things I've intuitively done (do). And speaking as a man who has been married for 34 years (as of this writing), there is nothing more valuable to me than my wife and what we've accomplished together (which of course includes our children). To all you men out there who wish for the same accomplishment, here's the book that can guide you how to achieve it.

—Dennis Lowery

Foreword

This is a happy book. It is also a serious book.

The author, Jack Carpenter, and his wife are my friends of several decades. Jack was the Best Man at my wedding to James J. Kilpatrick, a fellow syndicated columnist. Our union was a huge success because despite many difficulties we were good at compromising and hugging. When my husband died, Jack sang our favorite song at the memorial service. Such memories are important to nurture love and lasting friendship. And when the initial magic fades, good memories and small kindness keep us going.

Jack understands the complicated ways necessary to maintain healthy life's relationships. He's always creating new memories and experiences.

Because he practices what he preaches, he shares his ideas and observations in this book. His message is: leave the mean stuff on the global battlefield guys and pay close attention to hearth and home. That is where the heart lives and is happy. And he ends with a personal call to action. Make peace not war. It's not too late if you start today. It works. Honest.

- Marianne Means, Syndicated Columnist, King Features Syndicate and Hearst Newspapers (Ret)

Introduction

"Being deeply loved by someone gives you strength while loving someone deeply gives you courage."

—Lao Tzu, Ancient Chinese Taoism Philosopher (562 BC)

This book is for men. Married, soon to be married, dating or soon to be dating.

If you are in search of a supportive, fulfilling, and happy relationship with your wife or girlfriend, this is a good read for you. In fact, this book could transform your life.

Official Disclaimer

The author's style is a bit *off-beat* and *quirky*. Unique passages, nutty musings, and humorous stories appear without warning or clarification. The reader is best served by ignoring the superfluous and embracing the sublime. Whatever that means.

This book will challenge you to step boldly forward. Only the most courageous of you will.

Here is the task. I will offer ten suggestions in the next few pages. You select three of them to focus on and deliver the results to your wife or girlfriend for the next three months. If you accept the 3 for 3 Challenge and enthusiastically embrace it, you will improve your wife or girlfriend's happiness and yours alike. This will make your relationship more satisfying and fulfilling.

If it does not work, I will refund the purchase price of this book. Sounds daunting? Let us discuss a bit more.

First, you must make the dedicated effort to improve your marriage or romantic relationship. Without this first step, reading this book will hopefully be enjoyable, but that's about all. However, if you are dedicated then positive change in your life is very possible.

Years ago, I was a U. S. Naval Academy (USNA) Plebe (the equivalent of a college freshman) starting four challenging years as a Naval Academy Midshipman. Right away you could tell there were two groups of young men in my class (no women Midshipmen in my day).

First Group: Those who wanted to be there. We had all worked hard, endured test after test, were the Student Body Presidents, straight-A students in High School, football captains, and sports stars. Once classes started after Plebe Summer, we learned quickly how hard academics were while you had upperclassmen beating the stuffing out of you. Through hard work and unbounded resilience, we succeeded because we decided to. No matter the challenge. Things were never easy for most of us, but studying hard, learning how to be a Naval Officer or Marine, and graduating was our driving passion. Don't misunderstand, we had our college pranks, bad dates, wild adventures, new experiences, and crazy stories just like any college kid. However, we embraced the necessity to work hard and succeed whatever the effort. We decided to win.

Second Group: This group was equally, if not more, talented, gifted and qualified. The biggest difference was they were there because their parents wanted them to be there. Not because they wanted to be there. This is a bit of an overstatement. They wanted to 'try out' being a Midshipman. They wanted to give it a go and see what happens. If academics were too challenging, physical training too demanding, 0500 every morning too early, upperclassmen too mean (and they usually were), or they got homesick, there was always another college or university. 'Is this really worth it? I won't get yelled at by Upper Classmen at Harvard, Yale or Stanford. I can drink beer and chase pretty girls every night. And I don't have to march in formation ever again. Is this REALLY worth it?'

We lost almost half of my class through those four years at the Naval Academy. The clear majority of that half left because their hearts were not in it. They didn't want it badly enough.

Have you ever wondered why some couples are genuinely happy and others aren't? They're always on a fun outing. Golfing, playing tennis, hiking, beaching, or enjoying a sightseeing cruise. Other couples want to emulate them and enjoy the same smiles, laughter, fun, respect, adventures, genuine warmth and excitement.

Happy couples don't necessarily get all the breaks either. Many are not the most beautiful people and not the kind that graces the cover of People Magazine. Not all are millionaires. Many don't have waterfront homes on Maui. Some don't even drive Porsches and Bentleys (perish the thought).

So why in Heaven's name are they happy?

These happy couples are really in love, and the trials and travails of life don't seem to define them.

What about the unhappy couples?

They're like that second group I encountered at the Academy. Maybe they were 'there' in a relationship, for the wrong reasons or with the wrong person. But maybe they too are unhappy because they didn't want it—the relationship—bad enough.

This book offers ten suggestions that will transform your marriage and romance. If you follow three of these ideas for three months (3 for 3), I guarantee you will have a happier life with your partner. If I am wrong (and I am not), the book price will be refunded. That simple. Adopt three of these suggestions for three months, and you will be much happier. One other small requirement: you must tell your spouse or girlfriend what you are doing. You don't need to tell which three suggestions you have selected, but you have to get her assessment at the end of three months that things are better, worse, or the same. She needs to determine how successful the three months were. You will also assess, but her opinion is the guide. You must accept that you actually want your romantic relationship to work. You need to want it to flourish, grow, and be exciting. Your heart must be in it. Whatever happens over the next three months, you will not fail because you have chosen to succeed.

Decide that, and you are ready.

Since you can read this book in less time than it takes to fly from Washington D.C. to San Francisco and still have time to answer your emails, you will find this a light and easy read. I am not into big books so this will be short and sweet. Okay. Since you have decided to accept the 3 for 3 Challenge (or at least read the book), please jump on your virtual plane, put your carry-on in the overhead bin and briefcase below the seat in front of you, back away from the gate and let's go. Have a nice flight.

Are you sure you're ready?

I know you are.

Then, let's begin.

Suggestion One

"Girls just want to have fun."

—Cyndi Lauper

It's Supposed To Be Fun, Make It So

Fellas, this is the Holy Grail of happiness. Every woman puts fun at the top of her list of 'Must Haves' and 'Absolutely Needs' for a life of joy. Number one always.

It is highly likely that if you simply seek to have fun with your bride or girlfriend for the next three months, a whole new world of joy will follow. You probably don't even need to select the other two suggestions if you enthusiastically adopt this one. It is so powerful that it transforms the way you approach everything else. A big part of fun is the joy of experiencing new things and having new adventures.

Rather like the ubiquitous grade school question on the first day back from summer break: 'What did you do this summer?' No self-respecting grade school boy wants to answer that question by saying: "I pretty much sat in my room and played with my GI Joes and played video games all summer."

A much better answer would be: "My family and I went to Europe this summer. My favorite part was two weeks on the Côte d'Azur, the French Riviera. We visited Monte Carlo, Saint-Jean-Cap-Ferrat, Nice, Ville Franche-Sue-Mer, Cannes, and Saint-Tropez. And, WOW, you should have seen the swimsuits the girls wore on the beach! Not exactly like America!"

Now that's a fun answer to 'What did you do this summer?' If ever there was one! Those pretty school girls will really take notice now, at least for a few days.

That's the zest, newness, and freshness your wife or girlfriend wants from you.

Let's take a look at fun.

So, what does fun mean? Are you a fun guy? Are you funny? Do you tell a lot of jokes and stories? Are you a prankster that loves great April Fools hijinks? Do women want to engage you at a party and seek your advice? Do women smile and truly want to be with you? Are women comfortable with you and feel safe when you are around? Not all laughter, not all jokes, not all 'funny guy' stuff all of the time, but still entertaining.

However, if you aren't fun, or don't think you are, what should you do to become fun? What does fun really mean?

"Make me fun or give me Death." (Patrick Henry, 1775—sort of)

"Damn the torpedoes, full fun ahead." (Rear Admiral David Farragut, Battle of Mobile Bay, 1864—sort of)

"Fun, fun, fun, till her daddy takes the T Bird away" (Beach Boys, Brian Wilson, Mike Love, 1964—actually)

Curiously, I have interviewed countless lovely women (well at least five or six) for this book. And the number one reason a woman is attracted to a man is that 'He is fun.'

Not money, good looks, hair, car, biceps, *size*, washboard abs, vocabulary or number of teeth (applicable in some rural regions). Nope. It is fun. So, what is it? Why do some fellas master it, while others have a real problem? What are the key ingredients for a fun soufflé?

As Joe Pesci asks Ray Liotta in Good Fellas, "So you think I'm funny? What does that mean—Funny?" I would not recommend you engage your wife or girlfriend with the same psycho intensity of a Joe Pesci (no pen sticking in necks and eyeballs please), yet, it is a good question. So, what is fun/funny and why do five out of five women list it as number one 'must have' for love?

Webster defines fun as 'amusing, enjoyable, entertaining.' Everyone has their own cut on what fun is. Here is mine: Fun is seeking ways to make the other person happy. Wildly Happy.

For example:

Good Husband— "Honey, let's go to that new sushi place tonight."

Wife— "That's nice Biff, but I know you don't like sushi. Let's try the new Buffalo Burger place on King Street instead."

Good Husband— "I might not care for sushi, but you love it. They also have delicious Japanese beer there. I'll get rice and something deep fried. This night is to celebrate all you do for me every day. You'll have as much sushi as you can eat and we'll have loads of fun too."

Wife— "Thank you, Baby. That's really sweet of you."

OK. You just turned a simple night out into a special fun event for your bride because you made the conscious effort to turn a regular dinner out into a memorable event. You just created fun.

Well done, and a great example to follow.

How about this one?

Good Husband— "Babe, let's go to the Smithsonian this weekend to see their new exhibit of historical, hand-made American dolls."

Wife— "You know how much I love those. But I know you like historical cars, not dolls. As much as I would like to see the dolls, we don't need to go."

Good Husband— "Nonsense. I will make a picnic lunch with wine, bread, cheese, sandwiches, and fruit. We can Metro down, then Uber back to make it easy. We haven't gone on a field trip in a while. What do you say?"

Wife— "I say you are the best husband I ever had."

Good Husband— "Thanks. But, I am the only husband you ever had."

I really like this one because you both know the husband doesn't like dolls. Yet, he wants to do this for his wife. Genuine, selfless, and a nice move. Very well done, Sir.

That does bring up a fun-killer we should be mindful of. It is the penchant we men folk have to keep pushing and bugging to get more compliments from our wife or girlfriend for being nice to them. Here's an example:

> Insecure Husband— "Honey, I'm home, and I brought you some flowers."
>
> Wife— "They are lovely. Thank you so much for thinking of me that way."
>
> Insecure Husband— "Do you really like them? The florist says they are her favorites for this time of year."
>
> Wife— "Yes Honey, they're beautiful."
>
> Insecure Husband— "You know, I had to wait at the florist while she made up the bouquet. I'm a pretty important guy in my firm, to spend that kind of time."
>
> Wife— "Yes Dear."
>
> Insecure Husband— "And you know, I am giving you these flowers for no particular reason, just because I'm a good guy and you are my wife."
>
> Wife— "Thank you."
>
> Insecure Husband— "And I bet most other husbands never do these nice things for their wives."
>
> Wife— "Yep."

An insecure fella who had a great idea and meant well completely blew it by trying to get extra bonus points and compliments out of it. Very poorly played, indeed. Never beat your wife or girlfriend about the proverbial head and shoulders to get more compliments.

Let's try one more fun example:

Good Husband— "I know we both just got home from work, but let's leave the iPhones in the house, get a drink, walk down to the park and talk. We used to do that a lot, and have been too busy recently. Let's go back to that tradition and solve the world's problems together."

Wife— "I do miss those private sharing times. Sorry, we both get caught up in the silly stuff that means nothing. Great idea, let's do it."

You get the picture.

If she likes the floral arrangement and the cocktail napkins at a reception you both are hosting and you don't, approve her choices and give her a bouquet of roses too.

If she wants to relax in bed on Sunday, bring her breakfast in bed.

Embrace quirky fun stuff. Go back to where you first met and re-enact classic pick-up lines.

Revisit where you had your first dance, spin around the floor. Have your iPhone play that romantic tune you danced to years ago (as long as it is NOT anything from Barry White).

Pull out the wedding photos and see how thin you both were. Look at all that hair you had.

Smile. Be unconventional. Surprise her all the time. Seek her laughter. Take every opportunity to make ordinary events fun and enjoyable for her.

By doing these creative and exciting things, you are embracing fun. You may not be funny—like Joe Pesci—however, you are the personification of fun. And, most importantly, you are devoting time and energy to her. You do this, and you will be the life of your wife or girlfriend's party.

Don't pass this one up, my friends. It is the one thing that can totally transform happiness for both of you.

Suggestion Two

"You can't fake listening. It shows."

—Raquel Welch

Listen

What is the most important time of any day? Simple. The time of day when you say:

Good Husband— "Honey, how was your day?"

You know it has been a tough day for both of you.

Both of your consulting jobs entailed writing tough and complex proposals, one of your kids has an earache, one was kicked out of school for fighting. Your Mother-in-Law is coming to spend Christmas and New Years with you. The left front tire on her brand-new SUV picked up a nail and is leaking fast.

You know a good bit of the lay of the land even before you ask. So, after you ask the question, "Honey, how was your day?" What should you do?

What should you say? What should be your response to ameliorate all these challenges?

Answer: Nothing. Let the sound of silence and crickets prevail. Give your lovely bride or girlfriend carte blanche to talk. DO NOT interrupt for at least the first seven minutes. After that, a "Yes Dear" or two thrown in for affirmation is appropriate. But, you must sincerely listen.

Of course, if you want to make it all about YOU, try this:

> Bad Husband— (Let her speak for a minute then launch into) "Fine, fine, fine. Clearly, you had issues. Now let me tell you about MY horrible day."

Well Done. You have just re-emphasized and certified all the credentials for your hard-won title of Oafman. Faster than a speeding email. More powerful than an IRS letter. Able to leap over talking wives with single interruption and make it all about you. Oafman!

Perhaps there is another approach.

> Good Husband— "Honey, please tell me all about your day. Let me get you a drink and let's sit here in the garden to discuss. Just get it all out, Sweetheart. I am here to listen."

Then, listen! Actively Listen. Attentively Listen. It is NOT your job to offer solutions and answers for the day's challenges and problems.

Confused Husband— 'Don't offer answers and solutions. What do you mean? I'm a stud. I solve tough problems all day long. I'm the best at it. Why should I not help my wife when she's had a tough day? Why should I not impart my wisdom, experience, business acumen and knowledge when it would take me only a couple minutes to solve all my wife's problems? It will take her days to make the right decisions.'

"Danger Zone Will Robinson...." (Some Old Fake Robot in the original 1960s Lost in Space TV Show— sort of).

Men tend to internalize and analyze problems in their heads, while women tend to 'talk through' their concerns. When men hear something, we tend to compare that issue with our data bank of experiences that appear similar. If a pretty close comparison is made, then we have a good answer. If the question is almost exactly what we have dealt with before, then we have a match and the BEST answer.

All this superior cognitive reasoning is done without talking much at all. We men consider ourselves to be darn decisive and able to distill complex issues quickly into straightforward and proper courses of action without having to air matters in public. In other words, we men don't feel the need to share all our challenges, victories and defeats. That's why we men are definitely too cool for school (or so we believe).

Solving your wife's problems is NOT what she really wants. No sir. What she really wants is to be listened to. Now stand back from your throne of Solomon-like wisdom and that fancy Halloween costume Solomon-like hat and think about this.

She actually wants you to *listen* to her, not solve her problems for her. By you actively listening to her, she will find a way to work it out. I am certain you know (since you are the smartest person in any room.) that women have an abundance of Foxp2 Protein in their brains. That protein is a significant factor that drives the average woman to speak about 20,000 words per day. How much do men usually talk in a day? About 7,000 words. Let me get my calculator out and punch in those numbers. That's a whopping 13,000-word difference.

Women generally want to talk through their issues. Many times, in the talking process, women solve their problems just by verbalizing them. Talking provides an outlet for their anxieties and a great springboard for the decision-making process.

For example:

Wife— "I can't believe the partners want to send eighteen employees to the conference in July.

That is historically excessive, and I don't understand their thinking. Travel costs alone will be a few thousand for each attendee. Based on precedent, reviewing the attendance lists for the last three years, my recommendation would be to send no more than eight people. That comports with an increase from last year's one person but considers keeping expenses in line. But, I don't want to anger the partners, as I want to be a partner someday."

Bad Husband— "I had the same challenge a year ago, and it took me two leadership briefings and several heated exchanges to explain to the partners that we were not going to gain anything by sending too many people to the annual San Diego Conference. I researched all the historical data and presented an airtight case. And of course, after those heated discussions, throwing erasers, storming out of some offices and a couple bruised egos, the partners finally agreed. As always, I got my way and won the day."

Nice job Ace. You just made yourself the brash 'Star of the Show' again when this is about your wife or girlfriend. And you likely guaranteed your non-selection for 'relationship partner' to boot.

I know it feels as if we are actually helping when we offer advice. Normally, we are certainly not trying to be jerks at all. And many times our advice is exactly what the doctor ordered. However, just as many times it does not afford your wife or girlfriend the opportunity to solve big problems or issues on their own. Great decision-making by both man and woman, leads to better and happier relationships. Try this on for size:

> Good Husband— (After actively listening to the wife or girlfriend's concerns) "What do think is best, Honey?" (Of course, we know the husband or boyfriend has all the right answers ready to offer. Yet, he allows his partner to talk through it).
>
> Wife— "I think I will pull together a few slides and show the historical value of the conference regarding revenue leads and increased opportunity. Then my plan is to schedule 30 minutes with the partners next week, likely on a conference call. I can discuss my concerns with them and get their take on the right course of action. In the process, I might learn that they are actually correct and we should be sending more people. We'll see. And thanks, Biff. You really helped me by listening."

See how easy and effective that was? Just be quiet and pay attention. By doing so, your wife or girlfriend talked through the challenge and came up with a thoughtful, confident, and strong plan of action. She appreciated the fact you were a sounding board for her that enabled her to bounce a few ideas off you, with no judgment or assessment. You were there for her when she needed it. Well done, my friend. This approach elevates your wife or girlfriend's confidence and works every time.

Here's another example:

Wife— "Honey, you know how we focused on Elf on the Shelf for the last two Christmases. One of the best parts is the kids can't act-up or fight because Christmas could be in jeopardy. And they actually believe the entire myth that the elf returns to the North Pole every night to update Santa as to whether the kids have been good girls and boys. It has been wonderful and the kids still really believe."

Good Husband— "That's great." He then saw the concern on her face. "What's the problem, Honey?"

Wife— "Some kid at school told Jacob that Elf on the Shelf is not real and actually a trick by parents to get their children to behave."

Good Husband— "Pretty smart kid." He knew the minute it left his lips that he was about to get the 'that isn't the answer I'm looking for, look.' And he did.

Wife— "What should we do?"

Bad Husband— "Here's what we will do. I will find the kid who ratted us out and break his legs. Then I will visit his house with my chainsaw and cut down their Christmas Tree. Then I will take all their presents underneath that chainsawed tree and throw them out on the front lawn. Then, I will smile and say 'Have a nice day, you creeps.'" [Sometimes I actually LIKE the Bad Husband.]

Good Husband— "Wow. That's a tough one. Do you have a thought?"

Wife— "Yes I do. Find the kid who ratted us out and break his parents' kneecaps."

Good Husband— "You are my kind of girl, Sweetheart."

The point being, in this family 'crisis' you are deferring to her thoughts, plan of action, and recommendation. That builds trust and pride. Great job Good Husband.

Let's try one more example:

Wife— "Honey, I am really troubled. You know Josh has had some problems keeping up with the rest of his class. Since we are moving to San Diego at the start of his next school year, his teacher suggested we hold him back a year. Frankly, I am a bit embarrassed and worried about Josh."

Bad Husband— "No problem. Josh will outgrow his temporary stupid stage and become one of the smartest kids in his class. I was always the smartest kid in all my classes, and he is a chip off the old block. In San Diego, he will be the new kid in town and therefore a lady's man just like me. I don't know what you are so worried about."

Nice. Listen, Bucko. Your wife is really concerned, slightly embarrassed, and needing some help to figure out what is best for her son. You make it about your conquests as a smart, handsome, popular kid in school.

Let us try a different approach:

Good Husband— "Yes, Honey. That's a tough one. What do you think?"

Wife— "I believe we need to do the best for Josh, obviously. With a new start in San Diego, no one has to know we have held him back except the school administration. If Josh wants to tell his classmates, he can. But, if he just wants to be the new kid, he can be that too. I really don't like this, but I think it best if we hold him back a year. What do you say, Dear?"

Good Husband— "I completely agree. Let's talk to Josh after dinner and explain it to him."

Well done Good Husband. You let your wife talk through the issue. Result: the best choice for the whole family.

So, in review, the most important part of the day is her chance to explain 'What a day I had.' By listening and *not* jumping in with your solution, you are telling her:

1. We are equals and your day is just as (or MORE) important than mine.
2. I am interested in you as a person and not just a Roommate/Sex Slave/Pole Dancer/Bond Girl.
3. No matter what, 'I Love You, and I will always Listen.'

That is powerful, my friend. I have talked with some fellas who observe:

> Confused Husband— 'Hey my wife never listens to me, because she is always talking. I can't get a word in edgewise. Shouldn't she be

responsible too and listen to me? Isn't turnabout fair play?'

Excellent point, but he must not have realized or know what I mentioned earlier—about that 13,000 words per day difference between men and women. You must expect and allow for it. To those confused yet good men, my advice? Get a dog. They will always listen.

In summation, listening is powerful and worth the effort. I HIGHLY recommend LISTEN as one of your three choices. Try it.

SUGGESTION THREE

"Respect is one of life's greatest treasures. I mean, what does it all add up to if you don't have that?"

—Marilyn Monroe

RESPECT AND LOTS OF IT

When it comes to being happy together, few actual practices have as much positive impact as respect. Mutual respect is the foundation of a fruitful and happy relationship. It is the rock upon which you build your home.

You are proud of your own accomplishments, right? When you get a raise, promotion, an award, or win a tournament... don't these moments evoke pride and satisfaction? Of course, they do.

Are you just as proud of your wife or girlfriend and her accomplishments? Do you view her life and career as important as yours? Do you always take her phone calls? Is she the one you admire the most? While you are riding the train of success in your career, how do you view your wife or girlfriend?

Is she a passenger, a fellow traveler or a partner?

- Passenger—Along for the ride.
- Fellow Traveler—Along for the ride with some commentary rights.
- Partner—Equal shareholder. A seat at the corporate table. Joint decision maker. Co-Bosses.

A true partner can drive new enthusiasm, accomplishment, moral support, encouragement and can change the trajectory of your success taking it to new heights. You respect a partner in a firm because of their business acumen, experience, seniority, and position. So, how do we enable the compelling benefit of mutual respect in our own relationships?

First, you cannot fake respect. When you are at the store, or a party, or church, or a bar, or work, the way you treat your wife or girlfriend tells the story of whether you respect her, or not (and if you do not, how can you expect respect in return).

For example, I frequently introduce my brilliant and beautiful wife like this:

> Biff— "Please meet my lovely bride, call-sign 'MINK.'" [More on what a call-sign is and about this particular call-sign is explained later.]
>
> People— (Spoken in unison) "Oh, are you newly married?"

Biff— "Not exactly. We've been married for 21 years."

People— (Spoken in Unison, looking from me to my wife and back) "Oh, well, congratulations." [Though some may think, 'So why do you refer to her as 'lovely bride,' you idiot?']

What just happened?

By introducing my wife as my lovely bride, people immediately know:

1. I love my wife.
2. She is lovely.
3. I am proud of her, respect her, and people know it is not fake.

The women in the crowd are usually happy that a husband refers to his wife that way. Many have told me privately, "I wish my husband would show me that kind of respect. You really love the MINK, don't you?"

Most importantly, my lovely bride can always count on me to be the president of the MINK Fan Club. I am her biggest supporter, encourager, and advocate. And she knows it.

Body language is powerful too. Here's a case in point:

My lovely bride and I recently attended the black-tie United States Marine Corps Birthday Ball. Our guests were my president for sales with his lovely wife. Both are in their 40s, fit, tall, graceful and regal. In short—the 'Beautiful People.'

Throughout this fun and tradition-filled night with tall, handsome uniformed Marines and their lovely ladies, dinner, a concert by the president's own U.S. Marine Corps Band, and dancing, it was evident that my company president and his wife showed no interest in each other. Their eyes never met. No loving glances. No touching. No smiling. No admiration. No fun. No respect. When I asked at work the next Monday if the couple had a good time:

Company Sales President, "We loved it. Very impressive. Thank you so much for inviting us! A great, memorable and fun evening."

Blow me away. He showed no interest or respect for his lovely wife the entire night. Nor she for him. They looked as if they were attending their own wake. Or a trip to the dentist. Or a dinner of Meals Ready to Eat (MREs). Or a birthday party for a four-year-old. Or tent camping in the rain. You get the point, they looked like they had a terrible time. He could not fake respect for his wife because he has no respect for her. And she has zero respect him. I certainly hoped that they reflect, take stock in their marriage, learn respect for each other and eventually, turn their love around. In truth, their story has since gotten even worse with another pretty woman involved. I don't think they will be invited back to another USMC Marine Corps Ball by me in the near future.

So, how do you respect your wife or girlfriend?

Here are some easy early adopters you can do today (or the very next time you're with her).

1. **Open Doors for Her.** Car doors, restaurant doors, bar doors, church doors, home doors, hotel doors, Nordstrom doors, Tiffany doors. Opening doors set you immediately apart from the pack of regular fellas (hound dogs). It says you love her and that you are a true winner and a good guy.

Sometimes independent women will say:

Independent Woman— "That's not necessary. I am very capable of opening my own doors."

That is pretty much the same lie as –

Lying Wife— "I don't want a Christmas (Anniversary—Birthday—Valentine's) present this year. All I need is you."

Right. And, if you fellas believe that, then you probably believe Dennis Rodman is a great U. S. Ambassador to North Korea!

The point is, open the doors for your wife or girlfriend and they will immediately notice and appreciate. You will be the best, most thoughtful man on the block. Your wife or girlfriend will brag about you to her friends.

> Bragging Wife— "You know Biff has started to open all doors for me and be really nice too. It's just like when we were first married."
>
> Girlfriend Mates— "WOW. I wish my (Rip, Carl, Jeb, Thor, George, Tom, Santa, Donald) would do that for me."

Remember, it's about more than the door!

Let us go to number two.

2. **Say "Please and Thank you."** Good old please and thank you. We teach our kids to say it and sometimes demand it. However, do we guys do it with our wives and girlfriends as much as we should? Make no mistake, we indeed should! Saying please and thank you are great building blocks for a happier marriage and relationship.

How about this:

> Wife— "Honey. I just bought your favorite Scotch for you."
>
> Bad Husband— "OK."

Let's try that again with a good husband.

> Wife— "Honey. I just bought your favorite Scotch for you."
>
> Good Husband— "Thank you, Sweetheart."
>
> Wife— "And I want to have sex."
>
> Good (and Happy) Husband— "Thank you, Sweetheart!"

You see how easy that was? Everybody wins and has a perfect time too.

Try this one.

> Bad Husband— "Can we be intimate tonight, Honey?"
>
> Wife— "No."
>
> Good Husband— "Could we please have sex tonight, Honey?"
>
> Wife— "You bet Tiger, and I will bring the Scotch."

You can clearly see how "please" and "thank you" will ultimately change your life for the better. So, open doors, say please and thank you, and bingo... everything will change for the better.

3. **Give Her a Call-Sign.** Readers— 'What the heck is a call-sign? You're kidding me? Call-sign?'

"Playoffs? Playoffs? You kidding me? Playoffs?" (Colts Coach Jim Mora November 25, 2001—actual— after losing an NFL game with five turnovers)

It's easy. A call-sign is a name you generate for her, that you call her in public that connotes who she is and what she means to you. Call-signs are ubiquitous in the military, especially with Marines, Naval Aviators, and Air Force pilots. They are created by seniors, colleagues or juniors usually stemming from a personality, a birth place, or an event in life. Examples: "Stretch" (6' 7" Marine), "Wheels" (F/A -18 Pilot and Squadron Commander), "Lucky" (WWII Submarine Commander and Medal of Honor Recipient), "Big Foot" (launched off an aircraft carrier while standing on the brakes, popping all the tires), "Chesty" (Most decorated Marine General in history), "Electric Brain" (Admiral Ray Spruance), "Chappie" (Air Force General), "Hairtree" (Me as a Naval Academy Midshipman many hair follicles ago) are all well-earned call-signs.

They're bold, brash, fun, and always contain a refreshing nugget of truth and humor. It's also a great form of respect and admiration. So, what call-sign should you give your wife or girlfriend? What is tough, encouraging, unique and fun? What would she like?

What would her friends like? What would you like, and be proud of?

Let's go with a real example first then suggest some others. My lovely bride's call-sign is MINK.

Readers— 'Huh?'

Yep—MINK.

Readers— 'Why?'

Some brief background is in order here. My lovely bride recently retired as a Tier-3 Senior Executive (SES) from the Department of Defense. That is equivalent to the military's three-star admiral or general in seniority and in precedence. That means that when she arrives on the quarterdeck of a U. S. Navy ship, they strike eight bells to honor her. Her storied career is filled with accolades, and her reputation, tireless work ethic, leadership are impeccable. She is also a very nice person who demands superior results, on time work, fully vetted, concise, and accurate products. In short, while much beloved by all, she is actually a Velvet Sledge Hammer.

Hence MINK. Definition: Lovable, lovely, vicious. I refer to her all the time, in every event or party as the MINK. Our waterfront home is Mink Pointe, her Porsche's license plate is MINKSTR, our boats are MINK and Mini-MINK. You get the point. My lovely bride enjoys being one of a kind with her call-sign.

So now to you, my friends. To select the right call-sign, one that she likes, you like, and your friends are jealous of... you must 'profile' your wife or girlfriend to determine some immutable truths and exceptional qualities about her. I call this effort: Finding your True CS (Call-Sign). You must seek and find the unchanging certainty in your lovely partner, and select the one and only call-sign for her.

Here are some suggestions:

Ocelot— Beautiful, Sleek, Deadly.

Porsche— Fast, Elegant, Seductive.

Magnolia— Southern, Gracious, Stunning.

Osprey— Devoted, Innovative, Tough.

Bon Bon— Sweet, Delicious, Addictive.

Find your True CS and test drive it for a couple weeks. If she likes it, go with it. If not, ask for her help and select one you both like, then go with it. Remember, it is NOT a nickname, it's a call-sign. When folks ask how she got it, make up a story:

Good Husband— "An Air Force General met my wife at a dinner party and said: 'Biff, I am forever going to call your beautiful wife 'Stealth' because she is so mysterious, stunning and sleek. I know her name is Rachel, but, always, she will be Stealth to me.' So that's how my lovely wife got her call-sign Stealth."

She—your wife or girlfriend—will love you for it. You took the time. You did your homework. You came up with a call-sign you both like. Then, you created a backstory that fits perfectly (even though the story is a complete fabrication). This is respect. It demonstrates an enthusiastic commitment to your wife or girlfriend.

Respect is a super suggestion to pick as one of your 3 for 3. It is the cornerstone for long, abiding, happy relationships. If it's not present in both of you, then it's likely the relationship will go as this quote states:

"Marriage is like a deck of cards. In the beginning, all you need is two hearts and a diamond. By the end, you wish you had a club and a spade." —Unknown

SUGGESTION FOUR

"If you ever need a completely distracted, unfocused person who isn't going to listen to a word you say, I'm here for you."

—Unknown

DON'T INTERRUPT

I know you have been at a party and some wife or girlfriend is telling a story that goes something like this:

> Wife— "We had just flown into San Diego on United."
>
> Bad Husband— "Actually it was Southwest Airlines."
>
> Wife— "Well OK, Southwest, and we decided to split up, so Rip could get the Hertz Rental Car, and I would meet him later at-"
>
> Bad Husband— "It was National, not Hertz."
>
> Wife— "Fine, National Rental Car, and I would stay with the luggage at the terminal."

Bad Husband— "Honey—not the terminal. In the passenger pick-up area."

Wife— "Good grief Rip. The passenger pick-up area is in the terminal."

Well, you get the point. I don't know why couples frequently feel like they can interrupt their spouses to 'correct' a story when:

1. The listeners don't care.
2. It is not important.
3. The constant correcting of the story comes off like mere bickering.

Let us not pretend that only men use this irritating tactic. Both wives and husbands can be masters of the 'Screw-up a Great Story by Interrupting and Correcting' method of conversation.

Why? I am not really certain why people on both sides of the gender fence deploy this plan of action with their own spouse. Perhaps it is because it is One-Upmanship to tell the other spouse that "even though you are telling the story, I have all the correct facts" and, "I am in control."

Again, who cares?

So, what to do?

Inquiring Husband— "Should I just let my spouse free range with no fact checking? Just let her spin any tall tale imaginable? Let her confuse dates, time, place, trains, planes, automobiles, hotels, dinners, vacations, states, countries and names?"

You bet, you dunderhead. It is a story. Stories are made to entertain, to be told and enjoyed. This is her moment. If it is funny all the better. If it is entertaining, go for it. If it makes her feel good, bingo.

You want her to feel free to express herself. You want her to want you to be around when she tells stories. She wants you to lead the chorus of listeners as they smile, gasp, nod, laugh, and affirm all at the right times. You want her to know you are proud of her and her story telling prowess. Let her be center stage for once. All you must do is listen and sincerely agree. That demonstrates great respect for her.

I must digress for a second because I am completely guilty and quite ashamed about this next folly of mine. For years, I have had the tendency to respond with a 'me too, but even better' approach when my lovely bride has just been placed in the spot light because of a deserved accolade, a great story, or a unique moment in time.

Here's an example:

My Lovely Bride— "Honey, let me introduce you to our managing partner, Todd Renwright. Todd, this is my husband, Rip."

Managing Partner— "Rip pleased to meet you. A big thank you for allowing us to take so much of your lovely wife's time. She knows everything about our outstanding new Department of Defense customer. She is indispensable and the best hire I ever made."

Loser Husband Rip— "Well Todd, I am writing a book."

See what I just attempted? My lovely wife gets a tremendous compliment from the big boss, and I try to make the conversation about me. Bad husband. It took me a couple of those clumsy and inappropriate moments to learn that trying to change the subject to 'Me' is never a good idea. [M E are the first two letters of *mea culpa*, by the way.] Too much focus on making everything about you is not good.

Never interrupt a great compliment aimed at your wife or girlfriend with an 'all about me' deflection. Additionally, try not to fall into the ever-available trap of finishing your wife or girlfriend's sentences.

Example of wife talking to some folks at a cocktail party:

Wife— "I was dropping the kids off-"

Bad Husband— "At School."

Wife— "Yes, at school. When the German teacher Ms. Klaus walked up-"

Bad Husband— "To the car."

Wife— "Yes, yes. To the car. She asked me if our daughter-"

Bad Husband— "Jasmine. Our daughter Jasmine."

Wife— "Yes, yes. Jasmine was interested in-"

Bad Husband— "Interested in doing a Student Exchange program with Dickenson College. She'll get to spend the entire summer in Stuttgart with a family studying German. Isn't that great?"

Well, you get the picture. Not only does this tell your wife she is too stupid to finish her own thoughts, but it also will get you nominated for "Boor of the Year." You will probably win the election in a landslide. When you allow your partner to tell stories, receive great compliments, and finish sentences, you have empowered her to be happier, healthier, and more respectful of you.

How about another party example?

Wife—"Honey, you remember the time we went on vacation to–"

Bad Husband— "Tortola. WOW. Was that a wild time. That resort we stayed in was beautiful and the yummy eye candy around the pool."

Wife— "No Sweetheart. I meant San Diego when we had–"

Bad Husband— "San Diego? What are you talking about San Diego for anyway? We were just talking about Tortola."

Wife— "Actually Hon. I was telling the story about Point Loma and that great seafood restaurant–"

Bad Husband— "Why are you always changing the subject when I am telling a great story about Tortolla? I mean what is wrong with you? Why do you have to keep interrupting me? These people want to hear my story about the pool. "

The cow pasture-like aroma wafting from the Bad Husband pretty much covers it I think.

The 'Don't Interrupt'er' is an excellent device to have in your toolbox for a happier and healthier relationship. If you are somewhat of a 'serial interrupter,' consider this suggestion as a strong selection as one of your 3 for 3.

When you listen and don't interrupt, a whole new world can appear, and you will be rewarded by the one who loves you.

Suggestion Five

"There are only three things women need in life: food, water, and compliments."

—Chris Rock

Compliment Every Day

That great sage philosopher of our time, Chris Rock, with the quote above, hits it out of the park again. Compliment EVERY DAY. Or as author Rochelle Goodrich opines: "Compliments land as soft and gentle on my ears as a butterfly."

OK, Fine. So, what is a good, encouraging and much-appreciated compliment? They take many forms. I like to break them into three categories:

1. Physical Beauty
2. Intellectual Beauty
3. Measurable Accomplishment

Let's look at a few examples of each.

Physical Beauty. This one is powerful, always appreciated, and should be utilized as the number one weapon in the daily complimentary arsenal. Examples are:

Good Husband—

1. "Honey. Love your shoes. Your feet look especially tiny and delicate in them, just like Cinderella."
2. "Baby, your hair looks so pretty this morning. It has a beautiful sunlight quality to it."
3. "Darling, is that a new dress? Makes you look even thinner if that is possible. Or have you been losing a good bit of weight these last few months?"
4. "Thank you for being my beautiful wife. I love it when the fellas are jealous of me because of you."
5. And the always popular and ubiquitous "You look hot today, Sweetheart. Come here and give me a hug."

My lovely bride is an executive at a major consulting firm. She has many meetings with government leaders and required social functions to attend. Each time she dresses for an event, she walks downstairs and asks me:

Wife— "Does this make me look fat?"

Bad Husband— "Yes it does, Honey. Sorry, but I really have to be truthful."

What? Rewind the tape. ~~Bad~~ Stupid husband, ~~bad bad,~~ stupid, stupid husband.

Good Husband— "No. You look as lovely as a ballerina. Now let's take the bad husband out back and shoot him between the eyes."

Why does my wife want my approval when she is a big wig, highly respected, and gets compliments all day long from others? Because I am her husband. I am the one guy in the world she really wants to hear from and make happy. She seeks my approval and happiness because she actually loves me. This is powerful. Use that power well. Compliment her beauty, early, often, and always. Physical beauty compliments always work.

<u>Intellectual Beauty.</u> This may be a bit of a challenge for some of we men. Our beautiful wives can be more intelligent than we, but, that is darn hard to admit. We like to portray ourselves as smart, hip, and strong.

When your wife is just as smart, or smarter than you, it makes it pretty darn hard to compliment her on something that is sort of like a shock and awe, full frontal strike on the male ego. Here is a suggestion, when you have your "listening" time with your wife, that is a SUPER time to compliment her opinions on political issues, local issues, faith, and family. Even if those opinions do not match, respect hers as you would have her respect yours.

For Example:

Good Husband— "WOW! This North Korean thing, with their nuclear program mature enough to put a miniature nuke on a long-range missile, is bad. Very Bad! We need to lean more heavily on the Chinese to get Kim Jong Un under control. That's our last best hope, short of war."

Wife— "I don't agree. I think we're already past that and the Chinese have never been responsive. They seem content with what's become a dangerous status quo. No, I believe we need to put the pieces in place for reunification. The bloodlines between North and South Korea will be an irresistible force of unity and will obviate that Creep in the North!"

Good Husband— "Wow! That's pretty insightful, dear... and, tough too. I don't agree, mostly because I don't think the U. S. has the guts to make it happen. But, I respect your opinion. You are incredibly smart, my love."

Again, it's important that there is mutual respect even when you disagree. In the end— after the discussion, the disagreement and voicing of opinion—you want to walk away and still have lots of fun together.

Or, how about this approach?

Wife— "The Request for Proposal for the morale and welfare of Army troops is right up my company's alley. It may be a long shot, however, if we get the right partner, we have a chance to win. I have decided to write it up even though it will be a heavy lift. One thing for certain, you cannot win the business if you don't bid on it."

Good Husband— "I am so proud of you, Honey. You take on tough challenges like this one and have superior insight into possibilities. I think going after this proposal is a great choice on your part. You are definitely doing a super job for your firm, I am very proud of you."

Or, how about this one that affects all households:

Wife— "Honey, I have analyzed our Blue Cross Blue Shield medical bill for your recent anterior cruciate ligament (ACL) surgery. I think I now understand it. The hospital double charged the anesthesiologist portion and submitted it directly to Blue Cross Blue Shield for payment. Blue Cross rejected the duplicate charge because they already paid the real cost. So, the entire second anesthesiologist bill was passed on to us. WOW. That was a bruiser. I will call tomorrow and get this all worked out."

Husband— "Your new call-sign is 'Anne Sullivan' because She was the Miracle Worker for Helen Keller. Honey, those medical charges for my surgery are so darn complex, I could never figure them out. It's all Greek to me. Very well done, my Sweetheart. And, I adore you for all the intellect and problem-solving you show every day."

Appreciation and respect for her intellectual prowess demonstrate that you are keenly aware of her reasoned thought and decision-making acumen. And, that you're very proud of her for the complex ideas and facts she can put together to arrive at the best course for success. Powerful stuff, this is.

Measurable Accomplishment

Good Husband— "Honey, I am so proud of the fact you are such a SUPER mom, SUPER CEO, SUPER executive assistant, SUPER pastor, SUPER chimney sweep, SUPER hot mama, SUPER military member, SUPER domestic engineer, SUPER princess, SUPER wife, SUPER girlfriend, SUPER person, SUPER lover."

Or.

Good Husband— "Babe. I know you are very self-effacing but, let me tell you, that seafood paella you made for our dinner party last night was superb. Honey, I have never had better. Or, as delicious. Your delicate use of the Saffron and Rosemary plus the way you perfectly cooked the rice was fantastic. If I didn't know better, I would say you are a classically trained chef and not simply "someone who cooks." Very well done, Sweetheart. You are truly amazing."

The regular things our wives or girlfriends are and do offer a daily opportunity to praise measurable accomplishments. There are tons of them. The key is to listen and learn about the small routine accomplishments each day. Then, make a big deal about them in a way that elevates your partner.

Here are a few examples:

Good Husband –

1. "Honey, you did a great job on that report for the school council. So many Moms and Dads have singled me out to tell me."
2. "Honey, you were so kind to the White family after Sarah broke her ankle in the fall down their front steps. The food and flowers and real caring show what an encouraging neighbor you are. Thank you, my dear." "

3. "Honey, The Olde Towne Historic Board Chairman, Roger, said you are his "Tiffany Girl." Great job my dear."
4. "Honey, the way you worked the crowd at the reception last night was masterful. Very impressive."

Then, there are the extraordinary accomplishments our wives or girlfriends garner: Codified awards, bonus checks, podium appearances, promotions, special trips and all manner of public accolades. When your bride gets one of these, make a huge deal about it. Throw a party, take her out to dinner, give her flowers, grab a room at the Ritz, surprise her with some unusual gift. Make her the princess and you her standard bearer. Do this without fail, and you will be rewarded too.

"Wove, twue wove, wiww fowwow you fowevah and evah... So tweasuwe youw wove." (The Impressive Clergyman, The Princess Bride 1987–actually)

When she gets a big win, go over-the-top and make a memory for her that will last.

Winning Wife— "Honey. I just checked, and I have been upgraded to first class for my flight out to our Phoenix office. Do have any idea how that happened?"

Good Husband— "No idea."

Winning Wife— "Biff…."

Good Husband— "OK. Busted. It's just a small thing, but, I know you didn't want to go on this trip, and, you have been working so hard recently on the big Marine Corps deal you won, that I thought you could use a little pampering. Even if it isn't much."

Winning Wife— "Thank you, Baby. That is really not necessary and really nice too. Thank you, Sweetheart."

My dad who is now 94 and a WWII, Korea and Viet Nam Hero (with medals to prove) used to do a very cool thing for my mom. Every so often, dad would bring home an athletic trophy. (Like those given away for tennis tournaments, track meets, alpine skiing—you get the picture.) Engraved with words that heralded mom's super qualities (bubbly personality, great memory, great homemaker, highly articulate, very smart, very cute). Each unique trophy would have a special engraving like:

Trophy—'Prettiest Wife in Washington.' 'Carpenter Family Ping Pong Champion.' (Which she definitely was) 'Smartest Navy Wife Ever.' 'World's Best Mom.'

Mom absolutely loved these trophies because she was a fierce competitor and always wanted to win and be appreciated. The trophies themselves likely cost

$20 bucks or less. But, that wasn't the point. The point is dad went out of his way to give mom credit and consequently showed his appreciation and love which helped to get him out of a good bit of hot water, when he was not as complimentary or, took mom for granted. Smart dad.

Compliment. Praise. Encourage. Do not miss a day. You simply cannot compliment enough. With time, you will notice a perceptible and positive transformation with increased happiness for both of you.

Men, this suggestion works, so put it near the top of your 3 for 3 list.

SUGGESTION SIX

"I really don't know what's going on with you right now, but I'm pretty sure it has something to do with you being a Fucking Asshole." —Unknown

DON'T BE A JERK

This one is essential. It is as simple as can be, and yet it is such a common area where we can all improve. It is a 'Lighten up. Enjoy life and be fun,' kind of a suggestion. What am I talking about?

> Wife— "Honey, can you please take out the trash? The trash people come at 0730 tomorrow morning."

> Bad Husband— (Irritable and condescending) "I know that. You don't give me credit for anything. You treat me like a servant instead of your husband? Why do I have to do all the work around here?"

Has that ever happened to you? All your wife was asking for was for you to take out the trash. So why did the jerk in you emerge to give your bride a hard time? Likely because you had other things on your mind, or you hate taking out the trash, or you are sadly irritated or unhappy with your wife, life, circumstance, kids, job, golfing buddies, church, Pastor, Redskins, Seahawks, etc.

Imagine if you only said in an encouraging and supportive tone:

Good Husband—"Happy to, Honey."

In both scenarios, you still end up taking out the trash.

So, why be a jerk? Does it get you anything? Do you gain any points with anyone? Does it make you feel better? Why not go with being nice and not a jerk? I am certain your wife would appreciate it. And, it puts a star in your book that will shine when other circumstances (or something you've said or done) don't shine as brightly, and things turn unhappy. 'Nice' actually works. How about this one:

> Wife— "Honey. Can you please take Trixie to the vet Saturday morning? I promised to take the kids to the park this weekend and Saturday morning is the only time available."
>
> Bad Husband— "Hey. You know Saturday morning is unwind time in my man cave. We had to go to your Mother's Saturday morning three months ago, and I told you to keep those mornings open. Why do you purposefully try to

aggravate me? You don't listen, and you certainly don't respect me. Heck, I work my fingers to the bone all week, and this is how you repay me? Why can't you be nice anymore?"

That poor little Bitchy Husband. I wonder if he has his full Barbie doll collection in his man cave, or, just the ones in cheerleader outfits and swimsuits. Is Baywatch on a continuous broadcast loop in the cave?

How about this, after being asked to take the dog to the vet?

Good Husband— "You bet Honey. And after the dog is all set and you finish with the kids at the playground, let's all go get ice cream cones downtown."

One final example:

Wife— "Dear, the girls and I would like to have a Girl's Night Out this Wednesday. The plan is to go to the Mandolin Bar and Grill, get tanked and hit on all the single handsome, hunky guys there. If we get lucky, we will go to their place and play. I might not be back until next morning. Please get the kids off to school in time."

Bad Husband— "Yes Dear."

Clearly, the Bad Husband has got other things (younger women) on his mind. He is a true JERK.

Good Husband— "WHAT? You are frigging kidding me, I hope. Otherwise, I am waiting outside the Mandolin ready to kick the ass of any young fella who is cozying up to you. And you know, as a retired Navy SEAL, I will kick his ass into the next county.."

Good man. And, oh by the way, NEVER cross a Navy SEAL, unless you want to get kicked into the next county.

There are a million ways to respond to any question, situation or discussion and you get to make a choice. The best way is to try a path of respect and kindness. Choose to interact with your default position as nice, not a jerk. Your day-to-day interactions with your wife or girlfriend will always occur. They are an essential part of building and maintaining the kind of relationship you (most men) want.

Now let us discuss the 'Dark Side' of this valuable suggestion. I have a few acquaintances (not friends mind you) who are ALWAYS negative.

'This' is bad. 'That' is bad. Their wife or girlfriend is 'stupid.' They are not pretty enough. They are always spending too much money. They can't cook like my momma. They are always late.

Bad Dark Side Jerk— "You know my wife thinks she has a good job, but she doesn't make half the money I do."

Bad Dark Side Jerk— "I can't be in the same car with my wife for very long, because all she does is talk, talk, talk and say absolutely nothing."

Bad Dark Side Jerk— "My wife always packs too much to go away on a trip. Why can't she be decisive and a smart packer like me?"

Bad Dark Side Jerk— "I guess my wife can schedule the simple things, but when it comes to real substance, she is not even as good as my executive assistant."

Bad Dark Side Jerk— "My wife used to be a beauty a few years ago, but, look at her now. How am I supposed to be proud of her when she looks like that?"

I'm going to insert something here by author Dennis Lowery (used with permission). It's something about relationships—how people treat each other—that he wrote for his daughters and I think it's valuable advice to offer here:

ABOUT BEING GOOD... TO OTHERS by Dennis Lowery

One of my daughters once wrote something that I both admired and had a bit of worry over (it was in response to one of her friends who asked, *where are the good people?*). I'll paste the part that concerned me here:

"Helping people is what I love to do, I will never tire of it because there is always someone out there who deserves a helping hand. I have been raised by two loving and inspirational parents who have taught me to do the best I can with the hand I have been dealt. I am strong because of my family and loved ones, and I will use my strength to help those I can, in any way I possibly can, because I have faith in people, in us as a race."

I love that she is such a kind person. *But as her father and someone who has been far down the rough dirt—the real—road of life, I wrote this for her (and my other three daughters). But it applies to everyone young and old:*

There are countless good people in the world. Many of them surround me. Genuinely good people—the kind you want to associate with—

know there are other good people out there. It's the people that do not believe good exists you have to be wary of, and you absolutely have to be cautious with those you think might be good but seem to always need something... are always looking for someone to help them or to care for or about them. You will want to comfort these people... be a friend or possibly even a lover to them. You will want to be strong for them. But don't rush to do that out of reflex because you are so kind and good.

NEVER blindly believe a person is good.

Watch them.

Listen to them.

BUT, also see how they act when it seems no one is watching or listening to them. See how they treat others and most importantly, see how they feel about themselves (by their actions and words).

If what you see is negative... if their view of themselves is destructive, self-defeating or they are always running down or blaming other people and lamenting how their life sucks. Or conversely, they are over-the-top, overly enthusiastic about things (anything) when they surely don't have a basis to be that enthused and never realize their thinking is distorted or comprehend they have a skewed perception of reality. Be cautious.

Keep them at arm's length until they merit you letting them into your heart and your life. And if they don't improve, become considerate (of themselves and others), self-aware and rational, and continue with the way they are—keep them at a distance. Let them deal with their own life. You can be friendly with them but don't owe them any part of yours.

Making the terrible mistake to take them in, trying to help, to accept or tolerate them and keep a relationship with them, opens you up to their bitterness and bile. And they will eat away at your time and if it continues and you let it... their negativity or irrationality will affect your life. They can—through the smallest opening—drag you down into their dark hole. Don't let it happen. Only accept friends and relationships on your terms.

They have to prove to you that they are worthy.

They have to earn the right to your highest level of friendship or love.

The best way you can help people is by having confidence in who you are and in what you plan for your life.

That does not mean being selfish or self-centered.

It does mean you must be an independent thinker and above the very neediness, negativity and irrationality I just pointed out for you.

That makes you strong enough to protect yourself—makes you a truly good person—and the best kind of friend, lover, partner, husband or wife.

And that makes our world a better place to live.

I choose to have as little to do as possible with those acquaintances (and I do that without being a jerk to them) because they bring no value to those around me (and can, in fact, do harm). If you have people like that in your life (even on its periphery) heed this advice and make it an important principle to follow.

Back to wives and girlfriends: it is wise to always take the extra few moments to be kind and nice. It does not cost anything, it does not diminish your toughness and leadership. What it does do is show your thoughtfulness in all times and situations. As you enter this Jerk Free Zone, I predict within a couple weeks your partner will compliment you by saying:

> Wife— "Biff. You have been so sweet to me recently. You listen, don't interrupt me and are proud of me. And, you have been doing nice things around the house. I'm impressed. The kids are impressed. You are wonderful. The only question is: Who are you really? (Clint Eastwood, Pale Rider June 1985—actually)"

Well done big guy. You impress your wife or girlfriend by not being a jerk.

If you have a penchant for meanness, and you know if you do. No one needs tell you. Try this suggestion on for size. Give it a shot as one of your 3 for 3. For you, this suggestion may be the most transformative of all.

SUGGESTION SEVEN

"I'm tired of fighting. For once I want to be fought for."

—Unknown

HOW TO FIGHT FAIR

You know that into every lovely blue sky of happiness, some rain of disagreement and anger must fall. In other words, a fight. And you can bet, the way you handle a fight is much more important than any topic of disagreement or enmity. What do I mean? I mean fight fair. Have you ever heard of the Marquess of Queensbury Rules? Here is your short and only history lesson.

The Queensbury Rules for the sport of boxing were written in London in 1865 by John Graham Chambers, a Welsh Sportsman. The rules promoted sportsmanship and fair play. Before the rules, boxers would win at any cost (low blows, biting, kicking, etc.).

The rules were endorsed by Sir John Douglas, the 7th Marquess of Queensbury in 1867 (a Marquess is just below a Duke in royal—familial and bestowed—precedence) and now boxers had to 'Win by the Rules.' So, what are they? Pretty much all of the things you would expect: "No hitting below the belt, no holding, tripping, pushing, biting, spitting or wrestling." In other words, if you do not fight fair, you are disqualified.

Let's take a closer look.

I bet you there are some very private things about your wife or girlfriend that only you actually know. In many cases, things even her best friend does not know. Stuff like:

1. She is embarrassed about her poor grades in high school.
2. She had more than ten fellas before you met (sometimes many more).
3. She used to be fat.
4. She used to smoke.
5. She did not finish her doctoral thesis.
6. Her favorite rock group is Bread.

You know. All that really embarrassing stuff.

When you put the boxing gloves on and take your corners for a terrific fight, most are tempted to win at any cost. Just like the days before the Marquess of Queensbury Rules established the groundwork for a fair fight. However attractive winning is, do not resort to using secrets or past embarrassments as a viable weapon. Stick to the facts of current specific circumstances and keep it 'above the belt.' Address the narrow challenge and points of disagreement, make your case, and move on. Do not linger in unhappiness. There is no winning or losing in this, move along, my friend.

What am I talking about?

Normally, you both are really pissed off because of something the other has done, or said, or not said. Take it on directly. For example:

> Wife— "Why are you spending so many late evenings in the office with your team? You know, your team including that new beautiful marketing girl, Sharon? Why can't you come home at least a couple nights a week to have dinner with the kids and me? Why are you trying to ignore us as much as possible?"

> Bad Husband—What you want to say is: "Because I am shagging Sharon and she is gorgeous and hot. And, you made love to at least eighteen guys before we were married, so, what's it to you? And, I can't believe they would even want you because you smoked like a chimney. Plus, the fact you were 35 pounds heavier then. Why did I ever even start dating you?"

Yes, that would feel great, particularly if it was true, however, that is not a fair fight, Sir.

Good Husband— "Honey, we talked about the Carlson account. It is our biggest client in revenue terms, and I lead the account team. Remember when we discussed it, and I told you I would have to put in very long hours just to get the all-important presentation ready. Why don't we get a sitter, and you join me in the office for one of our late sessions? Then after we are through for the evening, we can go out together for some hors d' oeuvres and a couple drinks. We should be completed with the account presentation by next Friday. How about it, Babe? Are we OK?"

Wife— "You know, I would like that a lot. You sure it would be OK?"

Good Husband— "Absolutely. Everyone will be happy to see you again, and, you can give us your opinion on our approach to the presentation. I look forward to it, and you will be a great new set of eyes to critique us."

Wife— "Thanks, Honey, I would like that."

Brilliant. Taking a fight and turning it into date night. That's the kind of fair fighting that goes a long way to ameliorate the unhappiness of pugnacious words.

Or try this one on for size:

Wife— "Why don't you ever listen to me? I try to talk to you, and you run away, or get on your work computer, or find a reason to drive to the supermarket, or escape to a sandwich shop for a snack. Why can't we talk anymore? Why are you treating me like a second-class citizen? What is wrong with you?"

WOW. Them are fighting words. Those are words filled with long-term, pent-up anger, and sadness. Huge opportunity for a big course change, or a terrible mistake. At the very minimum—A huge fight. Many paths to proceed on this strong admonition. Here's one:

Bad Husband— "What are you talking about? I always listen to you. You talk too much anyway. Why do you always blame me for you being fat in college? I never should have given you the time of day when I learned you were dumb in high school and had lousy grades. What was I thinking? I am the most perfect guy you could ever find. Just ask any of my team at work or my friends. They all believe that you are a whacko to give me such a hard time. What is your problem, anyway?"

Uh oh. The Marquess would not be happy with that answer. You did not heed the rules of fighting fairly. In other words, too much past baggage, not directly enough addressing the genuine concerns of your wife or girlfriend. She didn't just create this complaint in a minute. It has been building up inside of her. By lashing out with old baggage, you have re-affirmed that you think she is stupid, hateful, and unloving. Not the best approach, methinks. How about this angle?

> Good Husband— "Sweetheart, you are right. I have been preoccupied with work and stuff. I have been ignoring you. And, when I first arrive at home after your work and mine, I need some quiet time before we launch into the events of the day. Please give me a good half hour to just be alone and depressurize. In that time, I can at least take stock of my own day and then be ready to be the partner you want. If you can do that for me, I will give you my undivided attention, which I know you want. Can we begin that new us right now? I love you so much, Sweetheart."

Or, here is another scenario. The often irrational 'I am just angry' moment that all wives or girlfriends go through now and then. And to be fair and honest, we men do this, too.

> Angry Wife— "I cannot stand my life. I was supposed to be someone that others admired and wanted to emulate. Now, look at me. My college friends would never recognize me. They

would think I am a spineless jellyfish. You have made me this way, and I hate you for it. How can I ever be of value when I am not even a little bit proud of myself? I hate myself."

OUCH. Pretty deep challenge, this one. Really tough—she is clearly feeling unloved, unappreciated and very not special.

Bad Husband—"May I suggest three nights alone in the Amazon Rain Forest to clear your head, my dear?"

Nice fella and a great husband. Well, perhaps this approach is a bit better.

Good Husband— "Honey, I know you are upset, and I can't pretend to fully understand everything you are going through. Why don't we go away for the weekend to a bed and breakfast in the mountains and talk about this entire unhappiness you are experiencing? I would most like to listen and let you tell me what is really going on. What do you think?"

Spot on fella, and well done. You answered the bell in a genuine crisis. Good luck and blessings on your bed and breakfast weekend away.

> Here is a wonderfully humorous take on a couples angry-*irrational*-moment that I think you'll find funny, and apt: *It's All About the Nail*. You can find it on YouTube by searching that title or at this link:
>
> https://www.youtube.com/watch?v=-4EDhdAHrOg

Now, let's try-on this perennial favorite (for those with children from ex-wives or ex-girlfriends):

Good Wife— "Honey. I see you sent your daughter a couple thousand dollars."

Bad Husband— "So, what's the problem? She has a roof repair issue and what's it to you anyway? You have always hated my daughter and been jealous. Is it because she is beautiful and was never fat or never smoked in college like you? And why are you so stingy with our money. You make a lot of money, but, so do I. We can never talk about money because you get so mad whenever it comes up. You are such a tightwad. And so mean; why did I ever marry you anyway?"

WOW. Did you read that Tsunami of Husband Hatred toward his Wife? All she asked was "Honey. I see you sent your daughter a couple thousand dollars."

And, he launched into a mean-spirited diatribe that had nothing to do with fighting fair and everything to do with a mean-spirited verbal assault.

If you feel the need to 'launch' into your wife, go take a walk. Feelings can be significantly hurt, and the damage can be long-lasting.

Of course, don't be a wimp. However, be a gentleman at the same time. Here's how it should go, your answer to a wife or girlfriend's question about sending money to your child from someone another woman:

> Good Husband— "I did, Honey." Even though I chose you over her mother—you're the one I love—I want her to know that I haven't 'unchosen' her. And that I love her, too, and will try to help when she needs and deserves it."

So, you get the point. Don't run. Don't hide. Don't ignore. Don't put it off. Talk directly to your bride about her concerns, explain your side of it and work something out. Fights are always going to happen as long as you are two different people. I don't like them, and they are tough to endure, but with them as a given, the best we can do is fight with rules that permit us to come out on the other side with dignity, respect, and closure.

Fight fair. No past embarrassing mistakes or memories. Don't try to hurt. Tackle head-on and get through the fight as soon as possible. Apologies are always a welcome balm to soothe the proverbial nicks and bruises. Best of all, it's a super time to make up with one another. There has to be an entire "The Art of Makeup After a Fight" book that someone should definitely write.

There really are no winners, ever. At worst, all must walk away with, *"It's only a Flesh Wound."* (Black Knight Monty Python and The Holy Grail, 1975—actually). Those wounds heal quickest.

If arguing is a big part of your relationship dynamic, I recommend this suggestion as a must in your 3 for 3 Challenge.

SUGGESTION EIGHT

"I did my push-up today. Well, actually, I fell down. But I had to use my hands to get back up so, you know, close enough. I need some chocolate."

—Unknown

GET OFF THE COUCH

I'm actually writing this chapter to myself. When I graduated from the Naval Academy, at 5'11" I was a strapping 155 pounds. I could bench press 225 and run three miles or so a day. Now, I am 210 and can bench press about 175 and bike three miles a day. What the heck happened?

Who pulled the ripcord on my fat suit? Who sneaked-up behind me and forced me to eat platters of nachos? Who gave me a lifelong supply of Guinness and made me drink it all? Do they make Speedos for fat guys? Wait. That's a scary thought.

So, what happened? All the usual stuff of course—53 years of 'heavy seas underneath the keel.' Too much great food, not enough jogging, walking and lifting weights. Too many Twinkies and, of course, too many single malt Scotches.

Actually, that sounds pretty darn great.

I guess that's why I did it.

But, if you have had to up your business suit size three times. You don't look at your fit and trim body in the mirror as often as before and, your lovely bride mentions Brad Pitt and Matthew McConaughey with increasing frequency. You may need to put down the Twinkie (or other cream-filled tasty snack cake) and get off the couch. I have a couple tips for myself. So, Self here we go.

Tip 1:

WALK.

Get up at 0600 every morning and walk with your wife or girlfriend for 1 ½ miles, or about 30 minutes. No jogging. No rollerblading. No skateboarding. No hot yoga.

WALK.

Pretend as if you are the morning paperboy or papergirl delivery team, and, you MUST accomplish the daily delivery every morning. Rain, snow, sleet and hail suck, however, you can dress to combat those great excuses. Walk every morning faithfully for three months and:

a. You will lose weight (likely five to ten pounds in three months).
b. You will have great conversations with your partner about EVERYTHING, including how much you hate walking this early in the morning.
c. You will look forward to your private time together, and even enjoy the walks. Each day will begin with a refreshing start, and you will definitely sleep better every night.

Tip 2:

Stop Eating White Stuff.

Yes, white stuff. For three months. What do I mean?

Eat meat, chicken, veggies, pork, fish, and Scotch. Do not eat pasta, rice, bread, white frosting, white Russians, white houses, or white horses.

Let me tell you after you cut out a white horse or two, you will lose at least 50 pounds. Guaranteed.

Here is the hardest challenge. You are out with a client, you order the supreme hamburger with no bun and a side salad. You are doing so incredibly well. Before any food arrives, the waiter says –

"Sir, we have our freshly baked sourdough bread and honey butter, which is, of course, our signature method of pampering our customers before the food arrives. The Wall Street Journal says our bread is "The Best Bread Ever." May I bring you a basket, Sir? No charge of course."

At this point, calm down. A couple slices of great bread with some delicious honey butter are not the end of the world. They are a treat. We all deserve a treat from time-to-time. Sort of like a visit to the Seahawk Cheerleader Camp as an honored guest. We earned it, and we deserve it.

Then, we must reset and get back to our 'White is not Right' program and remember we are getting more fit and hunky with every rejection of white stuff. Just don't completely fall off the wagon, because, the sawdust is a pretty darn hard landing. Don't eat an entire loaf of Wonder Bread in one sitting.

Aside from the award-winning bread, if you need to eat something white, do it on an aircraft flying at 30,000 feet or more. Everyone knows that zero calories can survive at that altitude. That's why all mountain goats are skinny, and all cows are fat.

Just the facts baby. Just the facts.

Tip 3:

Lift Weights.

Here is why.

- Promotes less fat body mass.
- Improves bones, strength, muscles and decreases injury.
- Improves image and quality of life.
- Burns a TON of fat. More than walking.
- Makes you feel huge.

All of that sounds pretty good. However, why should I try this inconvenient weight lifting thing?

Skeptical Man— "Hey, I may not be the fittest fella on the block, but, girls like me and my team and the VP of Sales think I am smart, funny, and with it. Why should I take the time to lift weights?"

Great question. I have a real experience and answer. After graduating from the Naval Academy, throw your hat in the air (I threw mine the highest of course), kiss your momma, shake your dad's hand, and you are off to new worldwide assignments. Assignments like submarines, Naval Aviators (both Navy and Marine Corps), surface ships, SEALS, Marine Corps Infantry and Artillery, SEABEES, Supply, and Logistics. One of my good friends and company mates at the Academy was Dan. He was on the tennis team and looked like an ordinary fella. Dan selected Navy SEALS as his discipline after graduation. Two years later at a party in San Diego, this broad-shouldered, muscular, fit guy walks up to me:

Broad-shouldered, muscular fit guy— "Jack, it's Dan."

Me— "Dan? Is that you?"

Dan— "Yeah, I know. I look at little different."

Me— "Not a little. A lotta."

Dan explained that he not only had incorporated pull-ups (hardest upper body exercise— ever), push-ups and crunches but also weightlifting—not heavy weights—into his three times a week routine. He jogged on his non-strength training days. Let me tell you. What a transformation. Dan went from normal everyday Dan to muscular, fit and confident Dan. That chance meeting changed my life. I have been lifting weights ever since.

So, when I say lift weights, I don't mean HUGE weights (40 pounds and over), I mean 20/25/30/35-pound individual weights (dumb bells). And, buy an inflatable big workout ball too. A standard routine takes about 30 minutes. Start with the 20-pound weights and slowly work up to the 25/30 and 35-pound weights with time. Accomplish three, 30-minute workouts a week for three months.

Each workout is simple and efficient. I have included my routine exercise that is refreshing, easy and works. The kicker is you actually need to do it. That is the only tough part. The workout itself is easy and fun. However, you must get off the couch and do it. Here we go.

a. Shoulder Press Seated. Sit on a stool or a chair with a straight back. Hold dumb bells at shoulder height, hands facing outward. Push directly (vertically) up. Three sets of eight.
b. Arm Curls. Three sets of eight.
c. Crunches on the big workout Ball. Three sets of 25.
d. Push-ups. Three sets of eight.

OK. That's it. Less than 30 minutes. You can accomplish at work, at the gym, in front of the TV, on business travel in the hotel gym or at your Maui waterfront house. Do this three times a week for three months, and you will look just like Arnold. Well, maybe not exactly. Probably more like Dan, but that's pretty darn good too. And most importantly, you will feel stronger, be stronger and more confident.

Your guns will celebrate your arrival into the "Ed Hochuli School of Guns" (NFL Senior Referee with HUGE arms). And, your partner will reward your new 'Bufforilla' appearance with gratuitous intimacy.

All for 30 minutes, three times a week for three months.

GO BIG. GO STRONG.

By the way, when you do the routine at your Maui waterfront house, please invite me to consult, offer on-site advice and provide motivation and emotional support.

Tip 4:

Trim the Trees.

What am I talking about? It is simple. Trim the trees, mow the lawn, wash the car, rake the leaves, chop the wood, spread the mulch, barbeque a great steak, hunt moose. In effect—be a man. Not a wimpy man:

> Wimpy Man— "Honey, please don't make me hunt moose again. They are massive, loud and have huge horns."

> Wife or Girlfriend— "That's OK Honey. I know how mean those moose can be to you. Why don't you go to the fabric store, pick out a nice Simplicity or McCall's dress pattern and sew a lovely new pastel dress for me?"

> Wimpy Man— "Thank you, Honey. May I go to my room now?"

I know a couple of 'Men' who think they are 'Real Men.' Yet, will not wash a car, trim a tree, chop a stick of wood, walk a dog, mow any lawn or take out the garbage under the guise they are a 'Real Man,' and that stuff is beneath them. I am actually impressed with these 'Real Men' because they hide behind the age-old fable that 'Boys will be Boys.' Meaning to show real work ethic and rational behavior would burst the bubble of their personification of teenage immaturity.

One unfortunate wife married to one of these toads says about her husband:

> Unfortunate Wife Married to a Toad— "Well you know that's just Bob. He doesn't do that kind of stuff."

Really? So, what 'Real Man' stuff does Bob do? Answer—NOTHING. Oh, he does love to go to expensive steak dinners, golf, drink heavily and smoke cigars. That is what 'Real Men' do, right? Clearly, this True Toad has no desire to be a True Man.

Don't be that toad.

Seek ways to do actual manly things for your wife or girlfriend. All these work-related activities burn real calories and a lot of them. Do good deeds and burn calories, great combination. Never give in to Father Time. Stay young, active, fit and funny. Make certain the boys in the office say something like this: "I hope I look like him when I get that old. He still has it."

In summary, put down the Twinkie and get off the couch has many desirable components:

1. Proper Diet

2. Routine Workouts—walking and lifting weights
3. Actual Manly Work

All these to make you more attractive, youthful, desirable and fun. There are many great things about selecting this suggestion as one of your 3 for 3 Challenge choices.

SUGGESTION NINE

"Leave me alone. I am only speaking with my dog today."

—Unknown

SPACE (THE FINAL FRONTIER)... GIVE HER SOME

Privacy. Time alone. Meditation moments. Rough day. Unhappy worldview. Cacophonous kids. Idiot boss. Road rage. Bills (Not Buffalo Bills). Busy schedules. Upset tummy. Bad hair day. Bad jokes. Feet that hurt. Head that hurts even more. WOW. Big stuff here. Men, we have been all been down this road with our women before. And it is not a pretty path. Haven't we tried EVERYTHING?

> Husband Trying Everything— "Honey, I know today has been rough for you. And, you seem a bit out of sorts. What can I do right now to make you feel better?"
>
> Out of sorts Wife— "You can go screw yourself and drink anti-freeze. I have no idea why I married you. You are invasive, buggy, mean, fat, insensitive oafish and a lousy barbecue guy."

> Husband Trying Everything— "Lousy barbecue guy. What the heck are you talking about? Are you psycho? I am the best barbecue guy in all the history of man. How can you say those terrible things just because you had a bad day?"
>
> Out of sorts Wife (crying) — "You don't understand me at all."

Stop the clock. Roll back and try this again.

> Wise Husband after out of sorts Wife blow-up— "Honey, I can see you have had a tough day. Unless you want to talk about it right now, I am going to give you as much private time as you want. I will take care of the kids— dog— maid— congressmen— exotic dancers— plastic surgeons— bill collectors: everyone. You just enjoy some private time alone."
>
> BINGO.

Or, how about this one?

> Good Husband— "Hey Honey. I'm home."
>
> Stressed Wife— *Crickets* [their sound the only thing breaking the silence]
>
> Good Husband— "OK. Well. Why don't you just enjoy some quiet time alone with a good Scotch while I entertain the exotic dancer."

Stressed Wife— *Crickets*

What a fabulous husband he is. The real key is to give enough time to your wife or girlfriend to permit them to work out her challenges.

> Stressed Wife— "Honey, my feet are cold. My head hurts. I just broke a nail. I hate my job. I hate my kids. I hate you."
>
> Good Husband— "Baby. Why don't you draw a bath and just relax for the next couple hours? I have the kids, and we will do mac and cheese for dinner. We also have a game of Monopoly waiting for us. I expect to see you at 1100 PM in bed."
>
> Stressed Wife— "You are the best. You are the Champion of Love" (Queen, November 1977— sort of)
>
> Good Husband— "Yes I am."

Fellas. When space is the right option for your situation, it is a beautiful thing indeed. I am so horrible at guessing what is troubling my lovely bride. I really can never tell. So, giving her time and space is—no bologna—the right thing. This suggestion takes almost no zero work. All you have to do is say you are giving your wife or girlfriend time, then actually be quiet and give her that time. There is also a spiritual component in this wise suggestion. When you give her time to be alone, meditate and be free from the whirlwind of daily events, she knows you are her soulmate, because you know her so well. What a genius you are. The sort of detached, distant, Go-Along Get-Along guy is now a soulmate. You are a tricky one indeed.

A more extensive and involved yet more comprehensive space option is to orchestrate and pay for a weekend with her best girl friend or friends. A real live example of this was a recent weekend when my lovely niece brought three of her best women mates for a weekend at our waterfront home.

> Lovely Niece— "Uncle Biff. I have a small group of three young mothers who would like to get-away for the weekend to discuss girl stuff. A weekend in a nice hotel would cost quite a bit. May we spend a weekend at your waterfront home?"

> Me— "Of course Lovely Niece. If you want us to be there to show you the ropes, take you out to dinner and host a reception in your honor, we are delighted to so do. However, if you want to just be alone, we will set that up, too."

> Lovely Niece— "Uncle Biff that is so nice for you to offer, but, we don't want old people hanging around to spoil all our fun."

OOPS. Actually:

> Lovely Niece— "Uncle Biff, our vision is to wear our jammies, curl up in front of the fire, eat pizza and just have a girl retreat to get-away and talk. Would that be OK?"

> Me— "Super. I will get you the keys, and our caretaker will give you a spin through the house and the grounds. Then it is all yours."

They all seemed to really enjoy their space and were effusive in their appreciation, and sincere 'thank you' sentiments for the weekend.

How about this one?

> Space Needing Wife— "I have spent the entire day in a New Hire class of idiots. I know that many are just out of college, but please, most can't find their way to the restroom. I know I have been with the company for three weeks, and, do know a bit more than these dunderheads, but, why do they need to ask me so many questions, during lunch, on breaks, in the restroom, in the courtyard—everywhere. I mean one helped me carry my briefcase this morning and must have asked me ten questions before I got to my office. I can't stand it."

Bad Husband— "Buck up dear and make my dinner. I am starved. I had a bad day too, and you never hear me bitch and complain. Grow up a little and don't overcook the Asparagus tonight, please."

OUCH. Hope that guy has a one-way ticket to Iceland (it will likely be waiting for him in the bedroom). Try this instead.

Good Husband— "Sounds like a really tough day, Sweetheart. How about you just relax with a glass or two of wine on the screened in porch and the kids and I will make dinner. You won't hear from us until dinner is served."

That man has a certain romantic future with his wife or girlfriend.

Space is a wonderful thing. You cannot go wrong with space. Contrary to what it means, it creates a connection that can bind a relationship together, which helps to get through the tough periods when things can look a bit bleak. Use it often and with sincerity. It is truly the final and best frontier.

"For small creatures such as we, the vastness is bearable only through love." (Carl Sagan— actually)

SUGGESTION TEN

"A Soulmate is someone who appreciates your level of weird."

—Bill Murray

LIVE LIKE YOU ARE COURTING

This suggestion is filled with the power of all the previous ideas in this book times two. After we marry or are engaged, some men (certainly none of we informed fellas) feel like:

> Some of Us Men— "Whew, glad that's over. That whole dating thing where I had to be nice the entire time. No letting my guard down. Always ready to be the kind of fella my girl expected and wanted. Man, was that a heavy lift. But now I've got that love and relationship thing behind me, I can relax and be the real me again. Man Cave here I come. Just like old times. Cheetos. Twinkies. Guinness. HOORAY."

Along with that feeling is the belief that we can now take the foot off the accelerator of our relationship and glide through life as before.

Men Gliding Through Life— "Let's see. I have had three business dinners this week. Almost no time for the family. I kinda promised the little lady I would take her and the kids out for some sort of outing this weekend. But, man do I ever just want to chill out in my cave. No shaving. Maybe I can have the family pick up some Popeyes Chicken. I can pretend that is the outing and I can stay here chilling watching the Golf Channel. WOW. I am so smart."

I know that can sound pretty compelling— always doing the minimum to keep everybody sort of happy, but, not really making it too exciting for wife or girlfriend/Family— Yet, that is when we slip into old patterns of:

1. Being less fun.
2. Listening less, talking more.
3. Showing less respect than we should.
4. Interrupting too often.
5. Forgetting to compliment every day.
6. Acting like a jerk for who knows what reason.
7. Fighting unfairly by bringing up old painful personal data points.
8. Eating white stuff, not walking, not lifting.
9. Give no space to our spouse and girlfriend.

This is when we run the risk of our marriage and dating becoming routine, like a business meeting.

And we can become bored. Stand by, my friend. That's when your Bride/Girlfriend zeros in on you one day and says:

> Troubled wife or girlfriend— "Honey, do you still love me? Or, are we growing apart? In fact, did you ever love me?"

"Danger Zone."—actually—(Kenny Loggins—Danger Zone— Top Gun— 1986)

Men. This is a clarion call to action. Your next moves are critical. It is the moment to have a real discussion with the person you love and figure out what is really going on. What we may find is that we unconsciously want our man cave more than our wife or girlfriend. In other words, our deeds betray us, and we are BUSTED. Our wife or girlfriend hope we will re-invigorate and refresh our love for them. Seek new adventures, new respect, new listening skills, new excitement. New places. New fun. So, in our busy lives, how do we do that, and keep all happy? A couple thoughts:

1. DATE NIGHT.

We have all read, talked about and hopefully experienced date night. Why? Because it works.

> Good Husband— "My love. There's that new restaurant in town called Taco Maco. One of my

sales team told me it is really great. Best margaritas in town. Why don't we get a sitter and go out this Thursday and try it, just you and me?"

Wife— "Love to, but I have the PTA meeting that night."

Husband— "OK. How about Tuesday next week?"

Wife— "Great. Thanks Honey. That will be fun."

Any kind of excuse to do something fun and unexpected with your bride is a date night. A movie, a play, a black-tie event, a gourmet dinner at home (with kids at a sleepover), an impromptu dance in the living room, a Dairy Queen frosty. As we said earlier, blast away on date night because it actually works. Use it often as a great pick-me-up.

2. PICNIC LUNCH.

Husband— "Hey Doll. I rescheduled my business trip to San Diego next week. That opens things up a bit. How about taking a picnic lunch to our waterfront park on Wednesday and enjoy some wine, cheese and French bread like we used to do in Ville France years ago?"

Wife— "Great idea Baby. I'll get some bruschetta and some sliced tomatoes too. This will be fun and send us down memory lane. We did have a pretty risqué time there didn't we?"

Husband— "I remember it well. Pretty steamy. No, really steamy."

That's my kind of picnic lunch: Steamy and risqué. The thing about picnics is they are very personal. You are not in a restaurant, or an airport, or a bar. You are one-on-one with the one you love. That makes picnics very intimate, attractive, seductive and compelling. Food, fun, conversation and a super memory making opportunity. One of my favorite picnics is a couple Subway sandwiches, white wine or champagne, your partner, and a blanket. Yummy indeed. I highly recommend picnic lunches as often as you are able. Many good things come from these special events.

3. REPLAY HONEYMOON NIGHT.

Husband— "Remember our first night of wedded bliss at the Ritz Carlton? You looked so beautiful in your exquisite gown, and we had a few folks over for a final champagne nightcap in our suite. I had a great time."

Wife— "Oh. You mean the wedding night when you had too much to drink and fell asleep as soon as your head hit the pillow? Is that the night you mean?"

Husband— "Yes, yes, yes. When are you ever going to let me off the hook for that extraordinarily romantic performance?"

Wife— "Never."

Husband— "Well, how about this? Let's dress up, go out to dinner at Le Refuge then check-in to our same Ritz Carlton Suite for a night of wild sex—just like our first night. In the morning, let's have room service breakfast in bed. Your sister can take the kid for a night, and we can be totally unavailable to the outside world. What do you think?"

Wife— "WOW. Looking forward to that wild night of sex."

Husband— "America is a land of second chances, you know."

This actually happened. All of it. Just let me say, the second time around was mucho miraculous, utterly memorable and a particular performance was a Top Ten List maker. Re-enacting the original memories of life can be very fulfilling and gratifying. A super mulligan if ever there was one. Tons and tons of fun too.

4. BEACH HOUSE ON MAUI.

Husband— "Hey Honey. Do you want to spend the weekend at our beach house on Maui? We can invite my buddies, Willie Nelson and Mike McDonald over for dinner and an acoustic jam session. Go to the nude beach and enjoy fresh sushi and poke every night for dinner, and Loco Moco and seared Ahi for breakfast. What do you say?"

Wife— "Can we go first class?"

Husband— "Sure Baby. Your wish is my command."

There you are. See how easy it all is? Since your Maui beach house is worth a couple million bucks, even non-first-class flight arrangements will work. She will enjoy business class just as much as first class, and you will save a ton of money. Although NetJets is not a bad way to fly either.

Naturally, few of us will ever have that beachfront vacation house on Maui. However, we can still do many other fun things together. We can replay courting memories with picnics, date nights, Ritz Carlton mulligans. We can pretend to go away to Maui and go to a local bed and breakfast and hang out in the hot tub all day. We can take an early morning hot air balloon ride with champagne, rent out a couple kayaks on a lake for the afternoon and explore new lake-front worlds with a drink. The key is to always be looking for a new adventure. In our home, we call it a MINKVENTURE. Adhering to the axiom 'All Things MINK,' we try to turn EVERYTHING into a new and quirky, memorable experience. Why? Because it makes everything more fun and enjoyable.

Even screwed-up adventures take on an aura of laughter and frivolity. All the hijinks, bad roads, bad flights, bad food, bad company (great band) are laughable and fun because you can make them that way. Your wife or girlfriend will think you are trying to win her heart anew. The payoff is fresh, fun and fantastic. Reclaim the happiness with your wife or girlfriend. You will be happy you did.

Closing

"One does not leave a convivial party before closing time."

—Sir Winston Churchill

If we have timed this right, you should be about an hour or so out of San Francisco and on your last Scotch before the flight attendant collects the glass. Have we considered anything new or different on our 2,419 Mile, five-hour flight? I think we have.

First, dating then being married to that extraordinary someone is a gift and joy. Sometimes we all get a bit stale and take the best things for granted. This tendency can lead us down a path of unhappiness and anger. However, if we desire, we can fully re-kindle the warm glow of the best days of that loving relationship.

This book offers ten suggestions that will help. If you select three recommendations out of ten and faithfully execute them for three months, I am entirely convinced you will reignite, re-boot, re-purpose, re-invigorate, re-create, re-build, re-up, re-energize and revitalize your relationship.

As a reminder, here are your 10 suggestions for your review:

1. **Have Fun.** The top requirement on every woman's list.
2. **Listen.** Actively, aggressively, intently, enthusiastically, purposefully.
3. **Respect and Lots of it.** Vital to our entire attitude about our wife or girlfriend and the way they view us.
4. **Don't Interrupt.** Give her the courtesy, respect and opportunity to speak for herself.
5. **Compliment Every Day.** Invent new and innovative ways to encourage her at every turn. Do not miss even one day.
6. **Be Nice, Not a Jerk.** Make everyday life as pleasant as possible. Default on the side of nice. Do not be mean.
7. **Fight Fair.** Marquess of Queensbury Rules apply. Do not dredge up 'old news' and upset her for no reason.
8. **Put Down the Twinkie and Get Off the Couch.** Amp up the energy.
9. **Space (The Final Frontier).** Give her space.
10. **Live Like You are Courting Again.** Bring back the magic.

We men can choose a few new approaches to encourage our wives and girlfriends, and make us happier too. For me, I have selected 'Have Fun,'

'Compliment Every Day,' and 'Put Down the Twinkie and Get Off the Couch' as my 3 for 3 Challenge. That challenge begins today. I will tell the MINK tonight over dinner and let the games begin.

I encourage you to take a risk and try three suggestions for three months. I definitely know you will be successful, but, hey, if it does not work, you get your book money back. But, if it DOES work, much lasting joy can come of it.

For example (And this just actually happened):

My lovely wife just returned to Reagan National Airport after a successful two-day business trip to San Antonio, TX. First time she has seen the Alamo and the River Walk. Busy but rewarding professional visit paid for by the client.

When I picked her up, I brought:

1. Two Dozen White Roses (COSTCO, $16.00)
2. Bottle of Ice Cold Korbel Champagne and two glasses ($12.50)
3. Leftover Barbecue Salmon and Chicken wrapped in Romaine Lettuce Leaves ($5.00)
4. Curbside Pick-up with our Mid-Sized SUV ($0.00)

Total $35.50

Reward—Priceless.

That's the point. It does not take much money to make every event fun and unique. The real key is to seek out innovative approaches to create new and unique adventures. Make every experience fun.

A Call to Action

"Even if you are on the right track, you'll get run over if you just sit there."

—Will Rogers

Here is the final deal. Tear out the letter (coming on a following page) and select three suggestions. Fold and put the letter in an envelope addressed to you. On the cover of the letter write 'DO NOT OPEN until XX/XX/XXXX (three months later than the day you filled out the letter).' Put the letter in your briefcase, sock drawer, gold bullion safe or secret sauce jar. Then focus on your three chosen suggestions with great enthusiasm and dedication for three months. Tell your wife or girlfriend you are trying three new approaches to mutual happiness for the next three months. Then, request her honest evaluation of results at the end of the three-month period. Good, Bad, No Change, Fantastic. 'The whole truth and nothing but the truth.' (Sworn Testimony under Oath—actual) Pursue these three suggestions with passion and honesty. It will be challenging, because, you will be self-conscious and wondering if you are doing the right thing.

Keep reminding yourself why you are trying this experiment. Don't get discouraged after the first week or two. Change takes time. Both you and your partner will go through fits and starts the next three months. It will not be particularly easy because it will not neatly fit into your present routine.

You may even be met with skepticism and a large helping of doubt. Keep the faith, baby. Your win is to see a demonstrable difference in your wife or girlfriend at the three-month point. The real success is you can be the recipient of a happier, more satisfied more encouraged wife or girlfriend. Perfect for all.

Hey Men, thanks for spending these couple hours looking at what may spice-up your relationship with your partner. At least I hope you have something new to reflect upon and have fun with too. The call to action is a clear one. Make the commitment to try it. Now tear out the letter and let's go.

"Just Win Baby, Win." (Al Davis, Oakland Raiders, 1963—actually)

CALL TO ACTION LETTER

I _____ do solemnly vow to do my best to succeed in improving my relationship with my wife or girlfriend by diligently working on the following three Suggestions:

_____ 1. Have Fun

_____ 2. Listen

_____ 3. Respect, and Lots of It

_____ 4. Don't Interrupt

_____ 5. Compliment Every Day

_____ 6. Be Nice, Not a Jerk

_____ 7. Fight Fair

_____ 8. Put Down the Hostess Twinkie and Get Off the Couch

_____ 9. Space (The Final Frontier)

_____ 10. Live Like You are Courting Again

Open this letter on (date) __/__/____. Request performance evaluation from wife or girlfriend.

Good Luck.

Afterword

As you now know, the author—Jack Carpenter—chose to treat the topic of love and relationships with humor and yet with honest and sage advice (in spots some of my own has been interjected). I think that approach works in the main thrust and believe it's the perfect tone needed to put things in context and to give some of the soundest advice possible when it comes to developing, maintaining and nurturing a relationship.

I know something about that. As a young man, I was a sailor and sowed my wild oats in places far and wide (domestic and foreign, across many seas) with ladies fair. But then I found the one that made the others pale in comparison. And so, we've been together for 35 years now, truly through thick and thin: early tough, lean times and days (into decades) of comfort and plenty.

With age comes reflection and with parenthood comes the desire to pass on what I've learned to my children (four daughters: two of which are adults and two that are approaching late-teens so, on the cusp of adulthood). Of course, a book… a guide such as this expressly intended to instruct on what women (be they wives or girlfriends) truly desire, is of tremendous importance to me. What's in this book is what I wish for my girls—how I want their partner, companion, boyfriend or husband to treat them.

Life. When we're young, it stretches out before us almost to eternity. At ten years old, 30 looks ancient. At twenty, it pushes back to 40; that's old to us. As we age, we slide that benchmark farther away from our current age because we realize it's all relative. It's something we learn along the way in life. We also learn about context and how that plays a larger role in how happy we are, or what we become...or fail to become.

And so, I reflect on my life. I think of what Thoreau said: "Most men lead lives of quiet desperation and go to the grave with their song still in them." I should modernize his thinking to include women. And modify to say that I'm not sure if most humans live that way. I do know that most of us have felt that at times in our lives and that, thankfully, it passed. But I also know that many do feel this way every day. They want... and worry that they'll never receive or get... they search and hope... and begin to despair and feel that they'll never find love. And their song—the hope for or reality of love—is dying.

Often, as we get older, we look for things to make our lives better, more meaningful. We prefer it to be a simple formula—a shortcut, an easy recipe; five minutes to a German chocolate cake that feeds a dozen people or in any situation just pressing a button to get instant answers. We buy cookbooks that support the latest diet fad because we want quick results. We go for the seven-minute workout, pushing a high-burn regimen into the smallest amount of time possible. That's all good and can work to make select improvements in our lives. But what we really want is the big picture, widescreen high-definition life that we dreamed of when we were young. Deep inside we still want this big, colorful life, no matter how old we are. But there is no seven-minute workout for the entirety of life; there is no quick, easy-bake solution for life; there is no simple formula for life. Life is about form and substance and in a figurative sense, it is performance art. Having the life that makes us happy and content can be quantified logically, but to make it manifest—make it a reality—it must be orchestrated and choreographed.

I know with absolute certainty that what you just read, if practiced, will lead to a better relationship now or one you find in the future. It can enable you to have a love that lasts, that brings you pleasure each and every day. And while the past can't be changed and you'll have to move fast to affect the present... with what you've learned from reading this book, you now have what you need to prepare for relationships in your future.

There's a moment in my short story *Wings* that captures perfectly an important realization. I'm going to share it here because it's apt and relevant:

> Not wanting to give her pity that would hurt more than her cuts and abrasions, he said. "In my life," stretching his legs he stood with a groan and a crackling of joints. "I thought I was trapped between what had happened and what could never be." He looked at her across the fire, the flames dance of light and shadow on the stone wall, as she sat with her head down. He turned his back to the fire and looked out into the night. "The road seems so much longer when we have no dreams to believe. And we have no destination... life has no purpose." He heard the steady sound of water running down the mountain and knew it would wear away more rock. "It stayed that way until I decided one day to start walking and not stop until I found what I sought." Turning around he stepped back to the fire and could see she was now watching him.
>
> "Have you found it?" She asked.
>
> "Not yet." He could hear the yearning in his own voice.
>
> "Why do you go on then?"

"Because." He smiled at her with knowledge that only comes from experience. "Because I deserve to find what I'm looking for."

No matter how you came to read this book. Whether some subconscious tickle prodded you to buy or someone thought it a fitting gift. I hope that you take the advice within it to heart and that you use it to find and hold onto the one thing that most humans are looking for that is most important. Love.

You deserve it.

Dennis Lowery
October 2017

About the Author

Jack cannot hold a job.

He was a paperboy in Hawaii, a very slow track star in junior high, a high school chainsaw expert on an admiral's estate (actually cut his co-workers leg in a moment of misguided daydreaming), a designer and maker/marketer of the Famous 'Vicka Soap' (his highly successful brother 'Dr. Zorro' was the brains behind this solidly fruitful enterprise, our neighborhood moms snapped up all our inventory), a public school refugee (Naval Academy and Naval Post Graduate School), a ship captain, a car salesman (Mercedes, Porsche, Audi and Range Rover) so a High End Slimy Sales Guy, a Reprographic (Copier) District Manager, Information Technology executive for several high and low-end companies, and a business owner.

No job was too simple to mess up.

But wait. Now, this 'book.'

Mostly, this is just one more attempt to succeed at something. So, please don't be shy. Purchase multiple copies with abandon. He will sign every one if you loan him a pen.

CPSIA information can be obtained
at www.ICGtesting.com
Printed in the USA
FSHW01n1037060218